JOSEPH MIDTHUN   SAMUEL HITI

BUILDING BLOCKS OF SCIENCE

ELECTRICITY

WORLD
BOOK

a Scott Fetzer company
Chicago
www.worldbook.com

World Book, Inc.
233 N. Michigan Avenue
Chicago, IL 60601
U.S.A.

For information about other World Book publications, visit our website at http://www.worldbook.com or call 1-800-WORLDBK (967-5325).

For information about sales to schools and libraries, call 1-800-975-3250 (United States); 1-800-837-5365 (Canada).

Library of Congress Cataloging-in-Publication Data

Electricity.
       p. cm. -- (Building blocks of science)
     Includes index.
     Summary: "A graphic nonfiction volume that introduces the properties of electrical energy. Features include several photographic pages, a glossary, additional resource list, and an index" --Provided by publisher.
     ISBN 978-0-7166-1421-0
     1. Electricity--Juvenile literature. I. World Book, Inc.
   QC527.2.E434 2012
   537--dc23
                              2011025720

Building Blocks of Science
ISBN: 978-0-7166-1420-3 (set, hc.)

Also available as:
ISBN: 978-0-7166-1463-0 (pbk.)

Printed in China by Leo Paper Products LTD.
Heshan, Guangdong
2nd printing November 2012

Acknowledgments:
Created by Samuel Hiti and Joseph Midthun.
Art by Samuel Hiti. Written by Joseph Midthun.

Dreamstime 22, 23; Shutterstock 16, 17, 20, 21

ATTENTION, READER!

Some characters in this series throw large objects from tall buildings, play with fire, ride on bicycle handlebars, and perform other dangerous acts. However, they are CARTOON CHARACTERS. Please do not try any of these things at home because you could seriously harm yourself—or others around you!

TABLE OF CONTENTS

There is a glossary on page 30. Terms defined in the glossary are in type **that looks like this** on their first appearance.

WHAT IS ELECTRICITY?

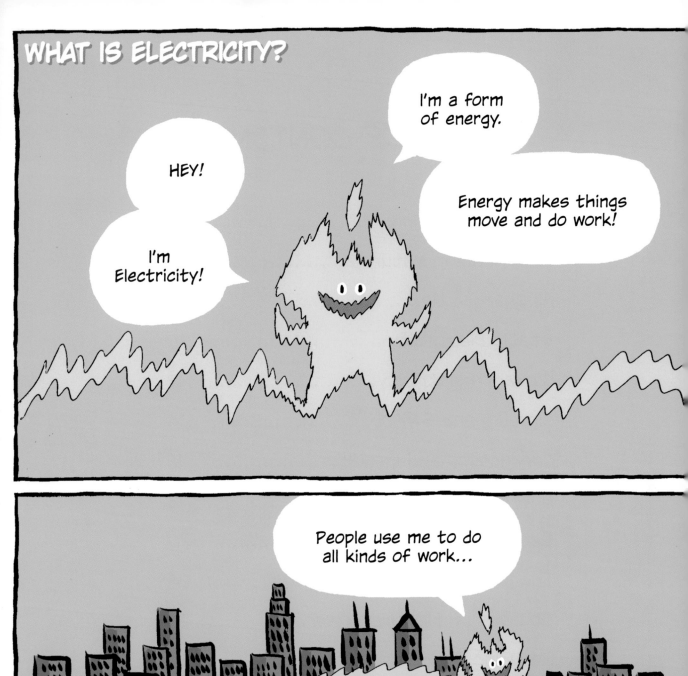

I power lights...

Electronics...

And many kinds of machines.

I even power you!

But you have to be careful around me. If you get too close, you might get shocked!

I'm inside you right now.

Every action and every thought are a result of electricity.

Electrical signals inside your body carry information to and from your brain.

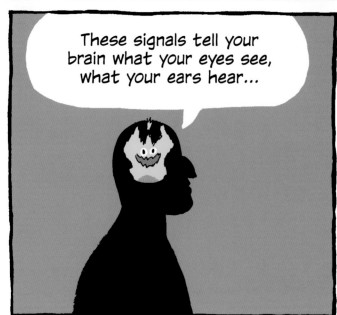

These signals tell your brain what your eyes see, what your ears hear...

...and what your fingers feel.

The signals even tell your heart when to beat!

PUM PUM

PUM PUM

7

All matter is made of tiny particles called **atoms.**

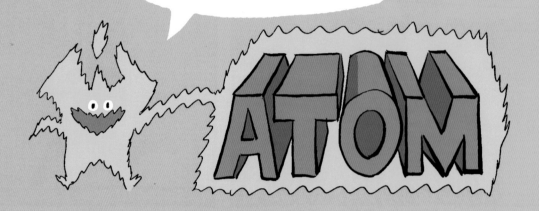

Atoms are made of even tinier particles.

Particles that carry a positive charge or neutral charge make up the center of an atom.

Electrons are negatively charged particles that circle around the center of an atom.

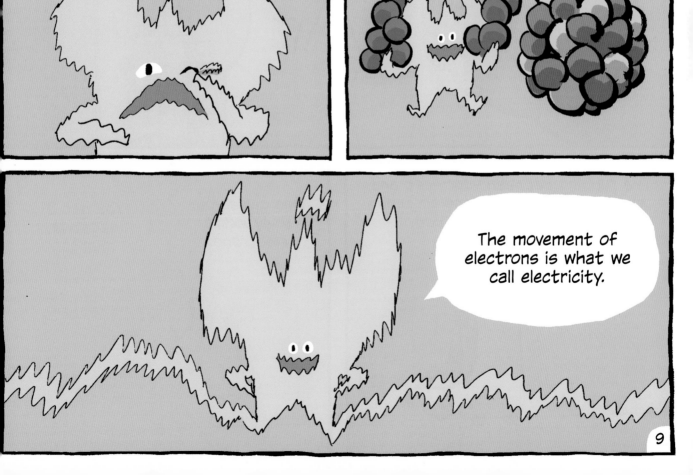

STATIC ELECTRICITY

The build-up of electrons creates **static electricity.** You've probably experienced static electricity firsthand.

Have you ever shuffled your feet across a carpet and then touched a doorknob?

Rub   Rub   Rub

What happened?

You probably got an electric shock!

ZAP

The rubbing between your feet and the rug causes electrons to jump from the rug to your body.

This gives your body extra electrons.

You get a negative charge!

When you touch the doorknob, electrons jump from your body to the object.

You feel this movement of electrons as an electric shock.

Electrons tend to move away from areas with a negative charge.

That's why they jumped from your body to the doorknob!

CURRENT ELECTRICITY

People can't use static electricity to power ordinary machines.

That's because the electric charge is released all at once.

To make electricity more useful, we must create an **electric current.**

An electric current is the steady flow of electrons from atom to atom.

Electric current that we use for energy flows in a loop called a **circuit.**

Think of a circuit as a raceway.

The cars are electrons that race around the track.

Simple circuits have three main parts: an energy source, an object that needs electric current to work, and a wire that connects them.

circuit

This robot uses batteries as an energy source.

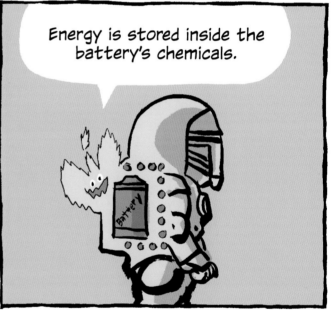

Energy is stored inside the battery's chemicals.

This energy pushes electrons through the circuit.

As the electrons flow, the robot moves!

CIRCUITS AND SWITCHES

In order for this light bulb to work, the circuit must be closed.

That is, it must form a complete loop.

Otherwise, the electric current can't get through.

LOOP

But what if you want to turn the light off?

You can use a **switch!**

Switches allow you to control the flow of current by opening and closing the circuit.

open

Switch

Flip the switch to "on," and the contacts are connected!

Closed

Switch

The circuit is closed. The light is on!

CONDUCTORS AND INSULATORS

Some materials allow electrons to flow more easily.

They're called **conductors**.

Many **metals** are good conductors.

That's why many electrical wires are made of copper or other metals.

Other materials stop the flow of electrons from atom to atom.

These materials are called **insulators**.

Wood, plastic, and rubber are good insulators.

Electrical wires are often covered by rubber or plastic.

These materials keep the electric current in the wire and prevent you from getting an electric shock!

GENERATING ELECTRICITY

So where, you might ask, does all this electricity come from?

People use lots of electricity every day.

Power plants!

Power plants use **electric generators** to convert mechanical energy into electric energy.

These giant machines are driven by a **turbine.**

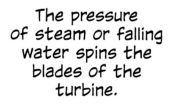

The pressure of steam or falling water spins the blades of the turbine.

The spinning blades cause magnets inside the generator to spin around a metal wire.

The spinning magnets push and pull on the electrons inside the wire.

The moving electrons create an electric current.

Power plants generate enough current to power entire cities!

Once an electric current is generated, it is directed into the electrical grid.

The electrical grid is a huge circuit.

It is made of power lines and connections that bring electricity to your home.

Your home is connected to the grid by copper wires wrapped in plastic.

These wires run through the walls of your home.

People tap into the grid by plugging a cord into an outlet on the wall.

Presto! The circuit is complete!

This led to the invention of electric devices, or electronics.

Some devices allowed people to talk across great **distances.**

Others helped people handle information quickly.

Over time, the demand for electricity grew.

Today, most people cannot imagine life without electric power.

But there are negative effects to all this energy use...

SOURCES OF ELECTRIC POWER

Most of the electric energy we use comes from power plants, and most power plants burn **fossil fuels**.

Fossil fuels were formed from the remains of living things that died millions of years ago.

Many people are worried that Earth's supply of these fuels will be used up.

On top of that, burning these fossil fuels harms our planet.

Scientists have learned how to convert energy from other sources as well.

For instance, this dam uses the power of running water to generate electricity.

And when wind turns the blades of a windmill, a turbine creates electricity!

Some **solar** panels convert the sun's energy into electricity.

Soak up those rays!

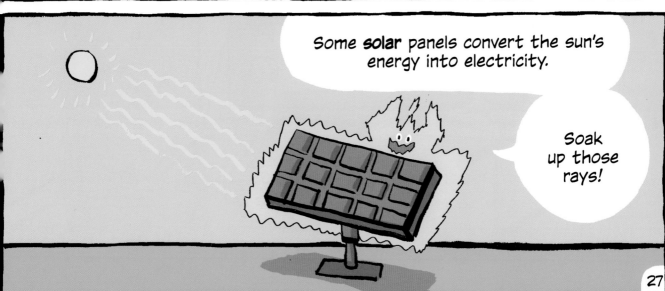

Or ask yourself, does the TV need to be on right now?

Look around!

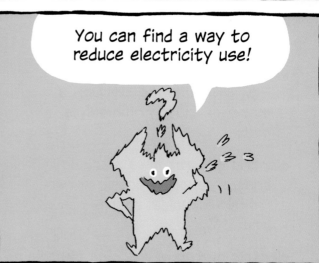

You can find a way to reduce electricity use!

Think about it!

And maybe *you* can come up with a better way to generate me—

Electricity!

GLOSSARY

atom one of the basic units of matter.

circuit a path for electric current. A circuit is usually made of metal wire.

conductor something that allows heat, electricity, light, sound, or another form of energy to pass through it.

distance the amount of space between two points.

electric charge a build-up of electricity.

electric current a steady flow of electrons through a material, most commonly a metal.

electric generator a machine that produces electric power from mechanical energy (motion).

electric motor a machine that produces mechanical energy (motion) from electric power.

electron a kind of particle that circles around the nucleus (center) of an atom. Electrons have a negative electric charge.

fossil fuel a fuel formed from the long-dead remains of living things. Fossil fuels include coal, natural gas, and petroleum (oil).

insulator something that prevents the passage of electricity, heat, or sound.

matter what all things are made of.

metal any of a large group of elements that includes copper, gold, iron, lead, silver, tin, and other elements that share similar qualities.

motion a change in position.

solar of the sun.

static electricity the build-up of electrons on the surface of an object.

switch a device that opens or closes a gap in a circuit.

turbine an engine or motor in which a wheel is made to revolve by the force of water, steam, hot gases, or air. Turbines are often used to turn generators that produce electric power.

FIND OUT MORE

Books

Blackout! by Anna Claybourne (Heinemann-Raintree, 2006)

Charged Up: The Story of Electricity by Jacqui Bailey and Matthew Lilly (Picture Window Books, 2004)

Electricity by Chris Woodford (Blackbirch Press, 2004)

Electricity: Bulbs, Batteries, and Sparks by Darlene R. Stille and Sheree Boyd (Picture Window Books, 2004)

Lightning: It's Electrifying by Jennifer Dussling and Lori Osiecki (Grosset & Dunlap, 2002)

Science Experiments with Electricity by Sally Nankivell-Aston and Dorothy Jackson (Franklin Watts, 2000)

Shocking Science: Fun and Fascinating Electrical Experiments by Shar Levine and others (Sterling Publishing, 1999)

What Is Electricity? by Lisa Trumbauer (Children's Press, 2003)

Zap It! Exciting Electricity Activities by Keith Good (Lerner Publications, 1999)

Websites

Benjamin Franklin: How Shocking!
http://www.pbs.org/benfranklin/exp_shocking.html
Recreate Benjamin Franklin's experiments with electricity at this website from PBS.

Edison Invents!
http://invention.smithsonian.org/centerpieces/edison/
In the late 1800's, such inventors as Thomas Edison learned how to put electricity to work. Learn about Edison's life and work at this site from the Smithsonian.

Exploratorium: Science Snacks About Electricity
http://www.exploratorium.edu/snacks/iconelectricity.html
Create batteries and start your own electric flea circus using these online experiments.

The NASA SCI Files: Electricity Activities
http://scifiles.larc.nasa.gov/text/kids/D_Lab/acts_electric.html
Experiments and simulations will take you into the shocking world of electricity at this website from NASA.

Physics4Kids: Electricity and Magnetism
http://www.physics4kids.com/files/elec_intro.html
Take a closer look at how electricity works at this educational website.

Power Up!
http://powerup.ukpowernetworks.co.uk/under-11.aspx
This educational website from the UK Power Networks teaches kids about electricity, circuits, and safety.

Tech Topics: Electricity
http://www.thetech.org/exhibits/online/topics/10a.html
Put together the basics of electricity, circuits, and technology at this interactive site from the Tech Museum.

INDEX